"Smart, expertly crafted, moving and ver

"Hnath has written one of this year's best plays . . . The focus is on the collision of viewpoints. Freedom versus responsibility, attachment versus solitude, domestic stability versus individual growth—these subjects are thrashed out in the explosive context of gender and social class."

— CHARLES McNULTY, *LA TIMES*

"Lucid and absorbing . . . *A Doll's House, Part 2* judiciously balances conflicting ideas about freedom, love and responsibility."

— ADAM FELDMAN, *TIME OUT NEW YORK*

"*A Doll's House, Part 2* displays real intellectual curiosity . . . Hnath makes an audacious Broadway debut with this pithy sequel. It delivers explosive laughs while also posing thoughtful questions about marriage, gender inequality and human rights that reverberate across the almost 140 years since Henrik Ibsen's original was first produced in 1879 . . . This taut, ninety-minute single act is as much an ingenious elaboration and deconstruction of *A Doll's House* as a sequel, and it stands perfectly on its own . . . With unfussy eloquence, *A Doll's House, Part 2* asks how much, in a century-plus, has changed for Nora and women like her in a world that often still has firm ideas about where they belong."

— DAVID ROONEY, *HOLLYWOOD REPORTER*

"Marvelous . . . Whiplash engaging and insanely entertaining."

— JEREMY GERARD, *DEADLINE*

"Mordantly funny . . . Endlessly stimulating . . . Fundamentally, and profoundly, serious: an exploration of our responsibilities to ourselves and to others; a dissection of the existential problems of marriage and intimacy; and a moving examination of the hard price that must be paid for self-fulfillment, today as much as back in the nineteenth century . . . Hnath's play is far too complex to be boiled down to a single apothegm, but it reminded me, at least, that if it sometimes seems impossible to live with people . . . it's absolutely impossible to live without them."

— CHARLES ISHERWOOD, *BROADWAY NEWS*

"Hnath uncannily unreels one inventive and plausible surprise after another in a text as fast-moving as the original is deliberate . . . Like Ibsen, Hnath explores the role of women in all aspects of life everywhere—and like Ibsen, he shines a light on the injustices done to women over centuries of belittling and underestimating condescension."

— Eric Marchese, *Orange County Register*

"Hnath writes fast, vibrant dialogue . . . Provocatively, the play functions as both homage and riposte . . . A forceful critique of self-actualization . . . A brisk and brainy sequel."

— Alexis Soloski, *Guardian*

"A great feminist comedy . . . Hnath provides enough ingenious structure to allow *A Doll's House, Part 2* to function quite smoothly as an often hilarious puzzle drama . . . Hnath is not using the preexisting characters and their backstory as ways of avoiding having to create something original; rather, they are springboards to something very new indeed . . . Hnath's play is at its core a public forum on questions of marriage that still bedevil us. Is wedlock ownership? May one love only once? How can people expect to stay together when they are always, individually, changing?"

— Jesse Green, *Vulture*

"The most thought-provoking play on Broadway . . . The strength of Hnath's drama is in its ability to get us to sympathize with all four of his characters . . . Hnath tackles not only persistent misogyny, but the cult of individualism, the compromises we all make for comfort, and the faith required to make a change."

— Zachary Stewart, *TheaterMania*

"Bracingly intelligent . . . Hnath examines the issues brought up in Ibsen's classic play with complexity and empathy."

— Terry Morgan, *Stage Raw*

A Doll's House

Part 2

A Doll's House

Part 2

Lucas Hnath

THEATRE COMMUNICATIONS GROUP
NEW YORK
2018

A Doll's House, Part 2 is published by Theatre Communications Group, Inc.,
520 Eighth Avenue, 24th Floor, New York, NY 10018-4156

The publication of *A Doll's House, Part 2* by Lucas Hnath, through TCG's Book Program, is made possible in part by the New York State Council on the Arts with the support of Governor Andrew Cuomo and the New York State Legislature.

TCG books are exclusively distributed to the book trade by Consortium Book Sales and Distribution.

Library of Congress Control Number: 2018032188
ISBN 978-1-55936-582-6 (paperback) / ISBN 978-1-55936-897-1 (ebook)
A catalog record for this book is available from the Library of Congress.

Book design and composition by Lisa Govan
Cover design by Monet Cogbill
Cover art courtesy of SPOTCO and BLT Communications, LLC
(Pictured: Laurie Metcalf, Broadway production)

First Edition, December 2018
Third Printing, April 2020

THE AUTHOR WOULD LIKE TO THANK:

Kimberly Colburn, Kelly Miller, Marc Masterson and
    South Coast Rep.
Kate Mulgrew, Tom Nelis, Tina Chilip, Mike Crane,
    Polly Lee, Peggy Scott.
Sarah Lunnie.
David Adjmi, Joy Meads, Marisa Viola.
Emily Morse, John Steber.
Tessa Auberjonois, Carmela Corbett, Steven Culp,
    Tracey A. Leigh, Lynn Milgrim.
Mia Barron, Rob Nagle.
Laura Linney, John Benjamin Hickey, Lois Smith,
    Grace Gummer, Daniel Sullivan, Lynne Meadow.
Elizabeth Marvel, Bill Camp.
Shelley Butler, Shannon Cochran, Bill Geisslinger,
    Virginia Vale.
Sam Gold, Osheen Jones.
Laurie Metcalf, Chris Cooper, Jayne Houdyshell,
    Condola Rashad.
Miriam Buether, Peter Nigrini, Jennifer Tipton, David Zinn.
Julie White, Stephen McKinley Henderson, Erin Wilhelmi.
Val Day, Derek Zasky.
Scott Rudin, Eli Bush, Joey Parnes, Sue Wagner, John Johnson.
Mona Pirnot.

A Doll's House, Part 2 had its world premiere at South Coast Repertory (Marc Masterson, Artistic Director; Paula Tomei, Managing Director; David Emmes and Martin Benson, Founding Artistic Directors) on April 9, 2017. It was directed by Shelley Butler. The scenic design was by Takeshi Kata and Se Hyun Oh, the costume design was by Sara Ryung Clement, the lighting design was by Tom Ontiveros, the sound design was by Cricket S. Myers; the dramaturg was Kimberly Colburn and the stage manager was Bree Sherry. The cast was:

NORA	Shannon Cochran
TORVALD	Bill Geisslinger
ANNE MARIE	Lynn Milgrim
EMMY	Virginia Vale

A Doll's House, Part 2 opened on Broadway at the Golden Theatre on April 27, 2017. The producers were: Scott Rudin, Eli Bush, Barry Diller, Carole Shorenstein Hays, Universal Stage Productions, the John Gore Organization, James L. Nederlander, Ambassador Theatre Group, Len Blavatnik, Peter May, Seth A. Goldstein, Heni Koenigsberg, Stephanie P. McClelland, Jay Alix & Una Jackman, Al Nocciolino, True Love Productions, Diana DiMenna, JFL Theatricals, Barbara Freitag &

Patty Baker, Benjamin Lowy & Adrian Salpeter, and John Mara, Jr. & Benjamin Simpson. The executive producers were Joey Parnes, Sue Wagner, and John Johnson. It was directed by Sam Gold. The scenic design was by Miriam Buether, the costume design was by David Zinn, the lighting design was by Jennifer Tipton, the sound design was by Leon Rothenberg; the dramaturg was Sarah Lunnie, the production stage manager was J. Jason Daunter, and the stage manager was Sherry Cohen. The cast was:

NORA	Laurie Metcalf
TORVALD	Chris Cooper
ANNE MARIE	Jayne Houdyshell
EMMY	Condola Rashad

NORA
TORVALD
ANNE MARIE
EMMY

WHERE

Norway. Inside the Helmer house.

WHEN

Fifteen years since Nora left Torvald.

THE SPACE

The play takes place in a room. It's quite spare. Some chairs, maybe a table, not much else. It ought to feel a touch like a forum. And it's crucial there be a door. A very prominent door to the outside.

Period, more or less.

In general, the whole play wants to move very swiftly, without breath, except where the play tells you take a breath or pause or silence.

A space between lines indicates a very brief pause or breath. Example:

NORA

And so I say, well just end it.
End marriage.

And it will end. I know it.

An ellipsis (. . .) in place of a character line represents a fuller beat. It's a moment of thinking or rethinking or sussing or a look, a sidelong glance, etc.

Enjambments are not meant to suggest a pause or break.

Dashes (—) within lines generally bring together fragments as if they are all part of one continuous sentence. They're not meant to pause the line. Rather, move through those dashes without air. Dashes at the ends of lines indicate an unfinished thought, either because a character halts herself or because another character interrupts.

Some lines end without punctuation. This is intentional and meant to indicate that there wants to be an almost seamless flow from one character's line to the next character's line.

Slashes (/) indicate the point at which the following character's line cuts in.

Nora

The room is empty.
And silent.
Silent and empty for a while.
Until . . .
There's a knock at the door.
Then silence.
No one comes to answer it.
Another knock-knock.
Nothing.
And another knock at the door.
From offstage we hear a voice call out—

Hold on! I'm coming!

(And then silence, until . . .
An older woman, Anne Marie, enters the room slowly—she's got a
little hobble.

She makes it to the door.
Unlocks it.
Opens it.
In the doorway: Nora.
Long pause.
Then . . .)

Oh Nora!

NORA

Hello Anne Marie.

ANNE MARIE

Nora I can't believe it's you!

NORA

. . . It's good to see you.

ANNE MARIE

It's really you. Nora Nora Nora—

It's been so long

NORA

it has.

ANNE MARIE

. . . You got a little fatter.
You got older and you got a little—

NORA

well you hit a certain age—

ANNE MARIE

Don't I know it.
Come in come here give me a hug it's so good to see you.

4

How are you. Come in there's some chairs you can take a
chair and sit in it

NORA

don't worry about me, I'm fine

ANNE MARIE

I'm going to sit I'm going to sit my knees aren't good
However I look on the outside—
inside it's all a lot worse. And how are your insides—?

NORA

They're good, Anne Marie.

ANNE MARIE

That's good.
Mine, I don't know, it's the stomach that
feels like it's gone all wrong,
but you look good and if your insides are all in order
then I'll take your word for it—

I just—I just can't believe it's really you

NORA

well

ANNE MARIE

I didn't know—no idea—if you'd ever come back around.
That first month, and those first six months—the first year or
two or three even—there was the thought that maybe you'd show
up, come back around, but then the more time that passed—you
didn't even write, no letters, nothing—

Fifteen years, fifteen years, could've thought you'd gone off and
died—

I for the record never thought you were dead—
a lot of people thought you were dead,
other people, not Torvald and the kids of course, but a lot of
people think you're dead.

NORA

. . . okay

ANNE MARIE

and I look at your clothes and it looks like you're definitely not
destitute

NORA

nope, not at all

ANNE MARIE

it looks like the opposite of destitute

NORA

I've done very well.

ANNE MARIE

That's just so nice. I'm happy to hear that, I never wanted bad
things to happen to you . . .

(Nora takes in her surroundings, moving her eyes around a room she
hasn't seen in fifteen years.)

NORA

The house is—

ANNE MARIE

yes—?

NORA

it's so . . .

ANNE MARIE

different?

NORA

from what I remembered

ANNE MARIE

same house

NORA

less stuff

ANNE MARIE

you forget things

NORA

there was a cuckoo clock used to be there, is that—?

ANNE MARIE

gone

NORA

the cabinet with the trinkets

ANNE MARIE

gone

NORA

and my piano

ANNE MARIE

that's gone too.

NORA

and there—a picture, a portrait—
there was a picture of my mother

> ANNE MARIE

I mean of course anything that was yours
got thrown out
after you left.

> NORA

. . . Right.
So, how much time do we have—?

> ANNE MARIE

until—?

> NORA

he gets back

> ANNE MARIE

a few hours

> NORA

you're sure

> ANNE MARIE

he's at work

> NORA

he still works.

> ANNE MARIE

But I had been thinking—I don't know how you feel about this—
I know you're just briefly in town—I know you said in your let-
ter that you were just going to be very briefly in town and so
I shouldn't tell the kids / that you're here—

> NORA

you didn't tell them did you—?

ANNE MARIE

no, I didn't

NORA

oh good, you scared me there—

ANNE MARIE

not that that would be such a bad idea—

NORA

they're grown up, they're grown-ups, they have their lives, their
lives are without me, there's no point—

ANNE MARIE

no, I understand

NORA

good

ANNE MARIE

but I mean if you wanted to see them, I'm sure they would really
like to see you, I think—

NORA

no, I don't agree—who am I to them? I'm nobody, they were
so young, I'm not a person to them, I don't mean anything—

ANNE MARIE

I don't know, I'm not so—well, that's aside from the point.

But what I *was* thinking is that maybe it wouldn't be a bad idea
to see Torvald while you're here, just to say hi,
just to, I don't know, see each other.
Given how much time has passed,

given how things ended,
given that you're just passing through,
no pressure, real easy, I just think
it could be helpful,
it could repair something

NORA

is something broken

ANNE MARIE

wouldn't say that, but—

NORA

you said "repair."

Is Torvald broken, still, is he still broken over me? I mean, I'm
sure he—

ANNE MARIE

no

NORA

good.
That's good.
So then—

He's well

ANNE MARIE

he's not broken, I didn't mean to make it sound—

NORA

yes, but—

ANNE MARIE

he's great, he's good—

NORA

he never remarried

ANNE MARIE

no

NORA

no, I didn't think so.

ANNE MARIE

. . .

NORA

. . .

ANNE MARIE

—but I do think he should get a dog.
I think if he had a dog he'd be happier,
not that he's not happy, I don't mean that but
he just likes dogs so much.
I see him—he'll see a dog
and he'll get so happy,
and likes to pet the dogs
and he lets them lick his face
and he holds them close.

I told him to get a dog and he said no and I said why,
and he said that dogs die.
Dogs die. They get sick, their bodies break, they hurt, and
when that happens he'd have to put the thing out of its misery:
cut its throat or break its neck or pelt its head with a rock,
and he doesn't want to come to love something
only to have to kill it.

I sort of wanted to say but didn't say but wanted to say that—
I think he's at a point where the dog will probably outlive him.
I think that's pretty optimistic to think that he'll be around to
put the dog down.

NORA

. . .

ANNE MARIE

But what about you, tell me about you,
what's happened to you?

NORA

I'll tell you what: I'm not the same person
who left through that door.
I'm a very different person

ANNE MARIE

yes, I'd imagine—

NORA

you really want to know?

ANNE MARIE

Yes I do, I know nothing!

NORA

Guess.

ANNE MARIE

Guess?

NORA

You want to know what I've been up to,
but I want to know what you thought I was doing—
what did you imagine—?

ANNE MARIE

oh Nora I don't know—

NORA

you must've imagined something—how could you not—
you're saying you never thought about it?

ANNE MARIE

No

NORA

you've wondered, you've thought—

ANNE MARIE

of course I—

NORA

what?

ANNE MARIE

You've done very well

NORA

you know that *now* but—?

ANNE MARIE

yes?

NORA

You thought I had a very easy time?

ANNE MARIE

No.

NORA

Go on . . .

ANNE MARIE

Okay well I thought maybe you might have had a difficult time,
being a woman and being the way women are sometimes—
often treated
these days

NORA

you'd think it would be hard

ANNE MARIE

that you struggled

NORA

and what would you think if I didn't struggle

ANNE MARIE

I'd think you were very lucky

NORA

lucky

ANNE MARIE

fortunate?

NORA

Not clever, not resourceful, not—?

ANNE MARIE

no of course I—

NORA

but first you'd think I was lucky.

Interesting.

ANNE MARIE

I didn't mean it as an insult

NORA

no I know, I'm just interested in these kinds of things, I think
it's to be expected that a person would think that after I left
this house
and my husband
and my children
that I'd have a very difficult time

ANNE MARIE

the world is a hard place

NORA

so we're trained to think.
I mean I think there's something in our time and place and culture
that teaches us to expect and even *want*
for women who leave their families
to be punished

ANNE MARIE

oh now I didn't say—

NORA

come on—keep guessing—
this is fun.

ANNE MARIE

. . .

NORA

Come on—

ANNE MARIE

feel like I'm being set up

NORA

I've done well.
So, knowing that I've done really well
what do you think I did that did so well?

ANNE MARIE

. . .

NORA

Go ahead.

ANNE MARIE

You've made money

NORA

right

ANNE MARIE

a lot

NORA

yes.

ANNE MARIE

. . .

NORA

. . .

ANNE MARIE

Are you
an actress?

NORA

(Scoff) No!

ANNE MARIE

A dancer?

NORA

Nope

ANNE MARIE

something
having to do
with
clothes?

NORA

I find it so interesting the kinds of things you're guessing

ANNE MARIE

alright then are you a lawyer—?

NORA

no

ANNE MARIE

a banker

NORA

no now make some serious guesses.

ANNE MARIE

. . . Do you make . . . things—?

NORA

eh sort of, yes and no

ANNE MARIE

I don't know, I don't—

NORA

you give up

ANNE MARIE

I give up.

NORA

I write books.

ANNE MARIE

You're a writer.

NORA

You're surprised.

ANNE MARIE

You've made money writing?

NORA

A lot.

ANNE MARIE

So you're a popular writer

NORA

women's writing is very popular, there's a big interest in—

ANNE MARIE

what do you write?

NORA

Books about women

ANNE MARIE

okay—?

NORA

and the things women do and want and don't want and don't do.
And the way the world is towards women
and the ways in which the world is wrong

ANNE MARIE

have I heard of these books?

NORA

one of them is really controversial

ANNE MARIE

I think I'd remember if I saw a book you'd—

NORA

I don't write under the name "Nora,"
I have a pseudonym

ANNE MARIE

oh that's clever

NORA

at first I wasn't sure what to write
so I wrote the first thing that came to mind
which was a story about a woman,
who lived in a house like this house
and had a husband like Torvald,
and lived in a marriage which—by all appearances—
was a good marriage,
but for the woman, for my heroine—
she felt suffocated, she felt like she had no options,
that her life was as his little wife and—that this was set in stone
and there'd never be the possibility of anything else ever.
And so she left her husband
and she started a life of her—

ANNE MARIE

so you basically wrote your own story

NORA

with some differences

ANNE MARIE

oh sure, but—

NORA

yes, it's mostly about me and
about how I no longer see a reason for marriage

ANNE MARIE

well now Nora—

NORA

also I think that women who are not happy in their marriages
should refuse to honor the contract
and leave

ANNE MARIE

that's a terrible thing to tell people.

NORA

Is it, though?
Think about it.
Marriage is cruel,
and it destroys women's lives

ANNE MARIE

oh I don't know—

NORA

really

ANNE MARIE

maybe in some cases—

NORA

more than some

ANNE MARIE

marriage makes a lot of people very happy, very—

NORA

that's debatable. I'd argue that most people would be happier, more fulfilled without it

ANNE MARIE

you can't say that

NORA

and you can't say that they wouldn't be.

ANNE MARIE

If marriage were so bad do you really think people would still be—after all this time of people living on this earth— would people still be getting married?

NORA

We do a lot of things that aren't good for us—
things we do because our parents tell us
from an early age—our parents,
our churches,
our leaders—
everyone
tells us that we need it, so we believe it,
and the idea gets etched inside our skulls
but you only think you need it because it's
all you've ever been told.

They tell us: "It's an expression of love,
the ultimate expression of love,
the one that we're all working towards"
—but how does that make any sense?—
to say, "I love you, therefore
you should tie yourself to me,
and you can never leave me,
you can never love anyone else,
you're off limits, I own you."
I *own* you.
That's what marriage says—to me that sounds
more cruel than kind—

also, also—

When people marry,
they say, "I choose you,
and I choose you forever,"
but who is this "you" that they're choosing?
Because people change, over time
people change into different people,
so how can you say that "I want
to be with this person"
when "this person" is not
going to be "this person"
three or five or ten years from now,
but there you are committed,
forever
till death
stuck,
stuck either with a person you don't want to be with
or with a person pretending to be a person they no longer are.
I mean, I'd even go so far as to say that marriage
makes a person change for the worse.

Because, before marriage, before marriage
you're wooing the other person,
wooing—what does that mean—that means
always putting your best,
your kindest, your most attractive side forward,
and you woo and you woo until
you can convince the other person
to commit to marriage.

And then what happens?
What happens when there's
no more reason to woo?—
to put your best side forward?
Marriage tells us that you're committed,
you're bound
to this other person
regardless of how you're treated.
Think about it:
Don't you think that that encourages
couples to treat each other
however they want?—to be as awful as you want—
it doesn't matter,
because you're in it until death.

This happens.
All the time.
And people are miserable.

Yes, yes, we want to be intimate with another person,
to know another person,
to love that person deeply,
and to be naked with that person—

but why do we need a marriage for that?

And why does it need to be with just one person
and for the rest of your life?

Seems so sad.

And we know it's sad—we *know* it—
we know it and we feel it
and we go and we *reach*
outside that contract of marriage,
all the time it happens,
men and women—
we fail to be faithful because deep down we ache for more,
because this ache is in the core of who we are—
but we stomp it out,
and we beat ourselves up
for failing to be something we never were to begin with.

And so I say, well just end it.
End marriage.

And it will end. I know it.
In the future,
twenty, thirty years from now,
marriage will be a thing of the past,
and those in the future
will look back on us,
and they'll be in shock,
in total—just awe—
at how stupid we are,
how backwards our thinking,
how sad it is
that we put ourselves through
this completely unnecessary
process of self-torture.

Twenty, thirty years from now,
people will have many spouses in a life,
even many spouses at once—
there won't be lines drawn between couples,
and there won't be jealousy because there won't be anything to
be jealous of

ANNE MARIE

but Nora—

NORA

you disagree

ANNE MARIE

all of this is just so—

NORA

it seems extreme

ANNE MARIE

and against the nature—

NORA

nature—what is nature—?

ANNE MARIE

that maybe there's a reason why things are the way they are,
why men are the way they are
and women are the way they are?
It's been like this for all of human history—don't you think
there's probably a really good reason why it's this way?
And you go and you fight it and that's going to make people
very uncomfortable—

NORA

I know. That's why at the end of the book she dies.

ANNE MARIE

Who?

NORA

The woman, in the book, my heroine who
says all the things I just said to you—had to kill her off—
Oh the book would have never been published
if she didn't die of consumption at the end of it.
I wish I didn't have to do that,
but I figured it's more important
that people hear her ideas than not at all,
and so—but in my mind it's not so much a
literal death as it is a symbolic one—
you know, she sheds her old life and enters into a new one.

And it's not like I'm saying anything that
anyone doesn't already somewhere in their minds
already sort of think—certainly if they're being
completely honest with themselves.

. . . which brings me to the reason I'm here.
You see—
some women who read the book were so moved by it
that they even went so far as to actually leave their marriages.
But it so happens that one of these women
was the wife of a particular judge
who presides in the particular city where I live.

He was mad and he wanted to find a way to ruin me,
so he set out to find out who I really was—
who I was behind the name I publicly use.

Turns out it isn't that difficult, all you have to do is
threaten to take a publisher to court,
so what?—who cares?—right?—
so he's got my real name: what do I have to hide.
And he went and did some digging around.
And after he'd done his digging,
I got a little letter from him,
and it said all the things you'd think he'd say:
"I know who you really are I don't like you I'm really mad"
and so on and so on
until
he revealed a secret that not even I knew.

He wrote:
"I know that your real name is
Nora Helmer."

ANNE MARIE

. . .

NORA

. . .

ANNE MARIE

. . . Yes?

NORA

That doesn't seem strange?

ANNE MARIE

That he found out your name?

NORA

But my name isn't Nora Helmer. Not Helmer. Not anymore.

Anne Marie, Torvald never filed the divorce.
Fifteen years ago, he was supposed to,
but he didn't
and now,
I find out that Torvald and I
are still husband and wife.

ANNE MARIE

I'm sure that's not true, someone's confused—

NORA

I didn't believe it at first either,
so I got someone I knew—a lawyer—to look into it, and
it turns out that, yes, Torvald never filed for the divorce,
and that, yes, he and I are still married.

Did you know—?

ANNE MARIE

no, no of course not.

NORA

This judge—he says that unless I publicly retract everything
I've said in my books,
write a letter and have it published in all of the newspapers,
apologize for what I wrote
apologize for encouraging women to leave bad marriages,
and say that what I said was wrong and dangerous—

that unless I do that,
he will expose me:
expose my real name,
expose me as a married woman
who claims to be unmarried—

I've signed contracts, done business, had lovers—all sorts of things that a married woman isn't allowed to do, that are illegal, that amount to fraud— This judge could make a lot of trouble for me.

ANNE MARIE

So *that's* why you're here

NORA

I do plan on seeing Torvald,
tomorrow I will see him,
and I will ask him for the divorce—
to simply send a letter to the local clerk,
just clear up any confusion,
and let everyone know that
we haven't been "man and wife" for the past fifteen years—
The clerk files the divorce—it's done. Crisis averted.

It's so easy for him to do it—easier for him than me—
the way they have the laws the man
can get a divorce for no reason at all
but a woman has to prove the man did something horrible to
her—threatened her life, committed incest, gave her syphilis.
Hopefully he'll just file the divorce and we can get it done before
the judge tries to follow through on those threats—

ANNE MARIE

and my role in all of this?

NORA

Based on even the little you said earlier,
it sounds like he's still upset about what happened between us,
and I might need your help.

(Anne Marie takes a handkerchief out and wipes her eyes.)

ANNE MARIE

Oh well shit. Shit Nora shit.

NORA

Are you crying?

ANNE MARIE

I think you've gone and misinterpreted what I said—
was it what I said about the dogs?—
and now you have this picture in your head of him being spiteful
and sad and broken and obsessed and—
I just wanted—oh fuck it all—I just thought it would be nice
if after all these years, you two could
sit together
and have a nice talk
and have things be normal
and nice
and maybe even, who knows—but
you read too much into the things I say.

NORA

Anne Marie. You didn't do anything wrong.
I might need a little more help.
We're allies,
we go way back—
you're like a mother to me,
you were practically my mother,
you raised me

ANNE MARIE

yes and I also raised your children.

NORA

And I'm like a daughter to you,
yes?
Isn't that true?
Before Torvald, there was you and there was me, and that was it.

ANNE MARIE

I don't like being in the middle of things—allies?—
that sounds like war.
I like everybody just fine—

NORA

yes, yes, but I am in a precarious position right now—

ANNE MARIE

so am I, Nora, so am—

NORA

yes, but if you—

*(The door opens.
It's Torvald.)*

ANNE MARIE

. . .

NORA

. . .

TORVALD

I'm interrupting something aren't I.

ANNE MARIE

Why aren't you at work.

TORVALD

I forgot something . . .

I left papers. I left—there's a big bound stack, like about this big that—I thought I brought it to the office—do you know what I'm talking about? I could've sworn I took it to the office, but I don't know—I feel like I'm—it doesn't matter.

ANNE MARIE

. . .

NORA

. . .

TORVALD

Who's your friend?

ANNE MARIE

. . .

TORVALD

Are you going to introduce me to your friend?

ANNE MARIE

. . . no?

NORA

. . .

TORVALD

Oh . . .

(He stares at Nora for a bit.)

. . . are you . . . ?

you aren't—

NORA

yes.

(Silence.)

TORVALD

You are.

NORA

I am.

(Silence, then . . .)

TORVALD

I have to go to the bathroom.

*(Torvald leaves.
Nora and Anne Marie, alone.)*

ANNE MARIE

I really thought he'd be out until late.
I didn't know.
I thought—he never comes home during the day, I
—you should go, I think you should go, you should—

NORA

No. You.
You should go.
When he comes back,
he and I will talk,
and when we talk,
we'll talk alone.

This isn't how I wanted it,
but this is how it is,
and I'll just deal with it.

ANNE MARIE

He might be in there for a while.

I'm pissed.

I'm pissed off at you.

I don't like how you've sprung this on me.

NORA

I have to deal with this now.
You should go.

(Anne Marie leaves.
Nora rearranges the furniture.
Two chairs, face to face.
After some time . . .
Torvald reenters.)

Torvald

A period of silence.
Followed by . . .

NORA

Are you going to say anything.

TORVALD

. . . No. I don't think so.
Not yet.

(And back to silence.)

. . . it's not not wanting to,

it's just that
I don't know what to say, really . . .

NORA

that's okay.

TORVALD

I did not expect this, I . . .

(Torvald sits, facing away from Nora.
Nora sits too.
Nora looks over at Torvald.
Torvald just stares out, straight ahead.
Nora goes back to looking out, waiting.
And so it goes on, more nothing.)

NORA

I'm fine just sitting here
with you
for as long as you want.

(Nora looks at him again, this time she holds her gaze.)

TORVALD

I've

thought a lot

about what this would feel like.

NORA

What.

TORVALD

This.

I'd wondered

what it would feel like if I ran into you on the street . . .

NORA

and how do you feel, Torvald?

TORVALD

. . . I feel shaky.

My hand is shaking.

My leg

is also shaky.

NORA

If you want

I can leave

—come back later. Alright I'll leave.

I'm leaving.

TORVALD

Tell me why you're here

NORA

maybe now's not a good time.

TORVALD

No, just do it . . .

NORA

Are you going to look at me?

TORVALD

I doubt it.
Not yet.
Just talk.

NORA

Alright.

Here's what it is, Torvald:

When I left you,
fifteen years ago,
—you remember that night—
I told you,
you're free. You have no obligation to me.
I gave you my ring,
and you gave me yours—

We agreed—we made an agreement—
that the marriage was done,
and you would divorce me,
and that would be that.

Fifteen years passed.

I've been under the impression all this time that we were divorced
until a few weeks ago
when I found out
that you never filed it.

TORVALD

. . .

NORA

Is that true—did you never divorce me?

TORVALD

. . .

NORA

. . . Why?

TORVALD

Did I want you to leave?

NORA

. . . no.

TORVALD

I didn't want to divorce you.
You wanted that.

NORA

Okay.

Well—

can we agree now that you'll
do what you need to do
to make the divorce "official."

TORVALD

And why do I need to do that.

NORA

I would do it myself
but I know you know that
you and I—
a man and a woman—
in the eyes of the law—
do not have equal rights to a divorce.
So I do need your help here, I can't do it by myself.

TORVALD

. . .

NORA

You know it's not right
to hold me to something
that I don't want
to be held to.

TORVALD

. . .

NORA

Are you really
after all this time
going to stand in the way of me getting a divorce?

TORVALD

. . .

NORA

It costs you nothing to do it.

TORVALD

You're assuming that it costs me nothing

NORA

what does it cost you—?

TORVALD

maybe not as much as however much that dress cost you

NORA

what—? Torvald—

TORVALD

. . .

NORA

Okay, then let me tell you what it costs me.
Because you won't file for the divorce,
because you're holding me in this marriage that's not a marriage,
you have made me a criminal—

TORVALD

a criminal

NORA

yes

TORVALD

How.

NORA

I've behaved as an unmarried woman,
I have conducted business that married women are
not allowed to conduct without the consent of their husbands,
signed contracts that are now void,
I could be prosecuted and put in prison
and believe me there are people who would have me prosecuted,
who would have me dragged through the mud

TORVALD

you're that unpopular

NORA

this doesn't just apply to me, Torvald.
This affects you, if you ever wanted to get married again,
haven't you ever wanted that—?

TORVALD

no

NORA

not even the possibility

TORVALD

no Nora, I haven't—you sorta killed that for me.

NORA

Well just so you know
there have been other men—after you, several.
I've had lovers.
I've had a life.
I did what I did thinking that you were no longer my husband,
and now, because you failed to take the action you said you'd
take—

TORVALD

I'm not sure that I—

NORA

I'm now in danger of having that life taken away from me.

TORVALD

. . .

NORA

. . .

TORVALD

You left.

You left me.

You walked out this door
and you left me
and you left the kids
and when I think back on what happened
I think to myself that I have one
big
regret:

I wish *I* left *you*.

NORA

. . .

TORVALD

I should have left you
long before you left me I should have—I think back
to all these moments where I should have left you—there are
so many—

NORA

are there—

TORVALD

—every time you chastised me for being too serious or being
too worried about small things, never taking seriously the things
that *I* cared about

—and every time you asked me for money—and every time you
asked me for money by first telling me how much you love me
as if by telling me that you love me would make me give you the
money—that's really manipulative by the way

—every time you'd ask me to do a favor for a friend of yours—
you had all of these friends, and always it became my responsi-

bility to fix their problems as if the only value I had in your life
was either my ability to give you money and find your friends
a job or a place to live—never considering the possibility that
maybe I didn't have time to help everyone you thought needed
help, or—

and you could tell that the favors you were asking me made me
uncomfortable, but you pushed and you pushed and you'd say
things to make me feel like I was being a wimp or weak

every time you talked down / to me—

NORA

you were the one who talked down to me

TORVALD

every time you flirted with other men—

NORA

I never—

TORVALD

yes, and every time you made fun of me in front of other men,
every time you rolled your eyes at me or—

NORA

you did that to me too, all the time you—

TORVALD

and when you told me that I was kind but being kind
wasn't enough to make you want to be with me
—and the moment when you told me that your own needs were
more important than taking care of your kids,
your own kids who needed you, who missed you,
who wanted you

—and then the moment you told me
you didn't love me anymore—
that moment that was maybe
a minute before you walked out of here—but I wish—
I wish I didn't take it like I took it.

NORA

. . .

TORVALD

. . .

NORA

Alright Torvald—I see that you see me as some kind of monster,
but you're not totally clean here either.
You've changed what really happened, in your mind.
You make yourself into the victim, the blameless, the right,
the better one of the two.
That's you. That's how you are—you
have to be right and superior.
This thing you do—this thing that men do of
standing in front of women
and looking down at them, telling them how the world works,
educating them, us, me
about how things should be
as if you were some kind of expert.

TORVALD

And what would happen if we—men—if we didn't—I wonder
sometimes about this—yeah, I won't disagree—it happens—we
do this, okay,
but I wonder if women don't ask that men behave the way we
behave, in some ways

NORA

really

TORVALD

if we didn't project some kind of confidence—an assuredness
in what we know or think we know—would women even be
attracted to men?—

NORA

confidence is different from—

TORVALD

to stand up straight and lead—

NORA

that's different from talking down to me.

TORVALD

How.

Explain the difference.

NORA

Also.

Also.

Here's another thing that bothers me:

You don't get angry.

TORVALD

Of course I do.

NORA

Maybe once you've ever gotten—

TORVALD

right now. I feel angry.

NORA

Right now.
You feel angry

TORVALD

damn right I—

NORA

I don't believe that you *are* angry, that you're in it, that you're inside of that feeling of feeling angry right—no, I think you're just outside of it, looking at it like it's some interesting thing.

You don't act.

You're constipated.

You're scared.

I don't like that you're scared—
it's a really big turnoff.

TORVALD

Sorry, I'm not trying to turn you on right now

NORA

and there it is

TORVALD

what

NORA

That tone

TORVALD

of

NORA

condescension

TORVALD

not standing up for myself?

NORA

Yeah, I don't read that as standing up for yourself at all.

TORVALD

Then what is it?
What is the difference between being
condescending and standing up for myself?
You won't say, even though I've asked you twice to show me—

NORA

so that you can just disprove me

TORVALD

so you can educate me

NORA

oh!

TORVALD

I would like to learn

NORA

you'd like to be right

TORVALD

I'd like you to stand up and take the lead
and teach me something

NORA

I did. Fifteen years ago, right here, I did that—

TORVALD

No.
No.
What happened fifteen years ago—if you'd like to talk about
that—okay let's talk about that—
is that you stood here and had your big epiphany,
and you know, I think—I thought then and I think now—
that a lot of things you said had a lot of validity.
You said that we never had a serious conversation in
eight years of marriage,
and yeah, I think that there was some truth to that.
We'd both been avoiding things,
avoiding hurting the other,
and all of that avoiding of stuff made us liars.
And yes, we have to tell the truth.
We have to stick our noses in some shit—
we have to—you talk about a true marriage,
you talked about how what we needed was a true marriage—

well, I think sticking our faces in the shit
is a really big part of that.

But listen, Nora, here's where you're wrong.
At the very moment that you realized the problem with our
marriage—

NORA

let's be real, there was more than one problem

TORVALD

no, I get that—I'm not saying there wasn't—but the moment
you brought the problems to light,
you walked out the door.

That's shitty if you ask me—

NORA

how is it—?

TORVALD

shitty?—because having epiphanies is easy,
but actually doing something about it is—

NORA

my "doing something" was leaving, that was "doing" and that
sure as hell wasn't easy

TORVALD

easier than staying and trying to tough it out with me—us
toughing it out together—instead you run off and pretend that
this is the same thing as being strong.

And I look at you and I . . .

NORA

. . .

TORVALD

. . . I think—

NORA

. . .

TORVALD

I did so much for you.
I loved you.
And you threw it away.

NORA

But who did you love really?
Because who I was when I was last here—that wasn't me.
You liked that, but what I was doing—that was just for show.
All the flitting around, the whole "oh Torvald, oh help me,
I can't figure out this or that, I can't do anything myself, oh help
me"—that's not me. That was a thing I was doing,
because if I didn't do it,
then you wouldn't have paid attention to
anything that was important to me.

I don't think you'd like what I'm actually like.

. . .

TORVALD

. . .

NORA

I hurt you.
I know that.
Don't think that I don't know.

And I knew what I was doing when I left you, and I knew what
I was doing was very cruel—very harsh. But staying would have
been cruel to me—

TORVALD

and our kids?

NORA

Don't bring up the children
as though that drowns out anything I have to say
about why I did what I did and whether what I did was right.

Do I wish I'd done it differently? Oh who knows.
Would I *not* do what I did? Absolutely not.
No regrets, Torvald.

TORVALD

. . .

NORA

I'm not playing around.

It's out of kindness that I'm asking you to file for the divorce and not me. It's easier for a man, the courts don't care about the reason, but for a woman to do it, the law asks me to prove that I deserve the divorce, and in order to deserve the divorce I have to make you look really bad—I have to ruin you—your reputation—in public record—I have to—I have to— Do you want that?

Torvald?

TORVALD

Do it.

Do it.

I'm not giving you a divorce because you don't deserve for this to be easy.

If you're going to ruin me, I want you to do it.
I want you to decide to do it.
I want you to do it so you have to think about what you're doing.

You say you'll ruin me,
you already did that,
except it happened while you were far far away.
This time if you're going to do it,
you're going to have to be part of it.

NORA

. . .

TORVALD

Alright that's what I have to say—
(Calls out) Anne Marie!

NORA

. . .

TORVALD

Anne Marie stop pretending that you're not listening and come
in here.

(Anne Marie enters, carrying a bundle of papers.)

I'm late.
I have to leave now.
Show her out when she's ready to leave?

ANNE MARIE

I found your papers.

(She hands them to him.)

TORVALD

. . .

ANNE MARIE

. . .

TORVALD

You and I will need to have a talk when I get back, okay?

ANNE MARIE

(Nods) . . .

(Torvald exits.)

Anne Marie

Anne Marie and Nora.

NORA
Alright Anne Marie, this is the point where I need your help.
Torvald won't give me the divorce himself, so now
I have limited options for how to get it.

Option number one is the option where I make up a story that
says that Torvald did something awful to me, threatened my life
or something and you corroborate that story. Option one would
work, but I would never do option one, because option one is
wrong and weak and it's just ugly and wrong and—

Option number two, I give in to the judge's demand, I retract all
my writings, everything I've ever publicly said about—everything—no, I'd rather die before taking it all back— Option two
is also not an option.

So what I need is an option three.

ANNE MARIE

. . .

NORA

Do you know of an option three?

ANNE MARIE

I'm still really pissed at you.

I think you should go.
He's gone, it's not appropriate for you to be here.

You've put me in a bad spot, you've put me in a . . .

Torvald is all I have in this world, my only family.
He takes care of me.
He supports me.
Do you know why?

He doesn't have to do it, the children are grown up,
but he does it because he's grateful to me
for sticking around after you ran off—
for staying with him through a very difficult time—taking care
of the kids—raising the kids—and looking after him—
oh he was mess!
You have no idea, you can't even begin to imagine.

The silence.
The not-eating.
The very dark thoughts he'd think.
The shame—

And how this must've looked to him—the thoughts he must've
thought when he saw us together, conspiring behind his—

NORA

we weren't

ANNE MARIE

I want you to go.
Just go.
Leave.
There's the door,
I know you know how to use it.

NORA

(About to say something) . . .

ANNE MARIE

. . .

NORA

. . .

ANNE MARIE

. . .

NORA

No, I'm not leaving.

I'm staying.

Get a room ready for me

ANNE MARIE

you're being selfish

NORA

it's my legal right / if I'm—

ANNE MARIE

No. No, / you're—

NORA

married to Torvald, I'm married to Torvald—I'm married to
Torvald then this is my house just like it's his house, I deserve to
be here, and this is where I'll stay until we're no longer married.

ANNE MARIE

Just take option two.

NORA

Never.

ANNE MARIE

So what—the judge wants you to write a letter taking back some
things you said that you probably shouldn't have said in the first
place—so what—it makes you feel bad, / just get over it

NORA

it's not about feelings—

ANNE MARIE

you don't have to run with every feeling you have, you don't
have to indulge—because some feelings make trouble—and here
I am—forget how I feel—I have feelings too, but also my liveli-
hood is at stake

NORA

so is mine—on paper we're married,
and that means as my husband
he has claim to all of it—
all the money that I've earned for myself

ANNE MARIE

he wouldn't

NORA

what

ANNE MARIE

take your money

NORA

maybe, maybe not, I don't know.
He was always very weird about money,
very controlling, very—

ANNE MARIE

you can trust him

NORA

but I don't want to have to trust him—that's my point—
I can't be tied to him.
I can't be always looking over my shoulder, worrying about—
That's what I left.
That's what I ended by walking out this door

ANNE MARIE

and what about me—?

NORA

what about you—?

ANNE MARIE

you're saying—what, that I don't matter—?

NORA

no, I'm—of course you—

ANNE MARIE

he'll kick me out

NORA

no he won't

ANNE MARIE

here I am, the one total innocent in all of this

NORA

is that so

ANNE MARIE

I think—

NORA

what makes you innocent?—

ANNE MARIE

aren't I?—

NORA

you're saying you have nothing to do with this problem?

ANNE MARIE

You're saying I—

NORA

you're not doing anything to help fix the problem.

ANNE MARIE

After all the problems I've already fixed for you
I have to fix this too?

Is that what you're really saying?

Fuck you, Nora.

Fuck you.

You have zero gratitude.
I raised your kids.
You should be coming in here—first words out of your mouth
should have been:
Thank you Anne Marie.
Thank you for abandoning your own life, your own child
and raising mine, so that I could go off to do my little thing.

NORA

I didn't ask you to do that.
I didn't make you stay.
I left.
You decided to stay.
I'm thankful that you stayed,
but that was not your responsibility

ANNE MARIE

but—

NORA

—was your choice, not—

ANNE MARIE

how could I leave

NORA

just like I did

ANNE MARIE

I'm not as cold as you.

NORA

You had even less reason to stay.
It should have been easier for you than me.

ANNE MARIE

It was my job, Nora, and if I didn't do what I did, three very young children were going to be left alone—

NORA

They had Torvald.

ANNE MARIE

A father but no mother?

NORA

Is that not enough?
Men leave their families—happens all the time—a mother but no father—
now, but if a woman—if a woman does it—she's a monster, and the children are ruined—

ANNE MARIE

far as I'm concerned, either way it's bad

NORA

also,
also—and I'm just gonna put this out there—you do realize that you kind of did the same thing I did—

ANNE MARIE

How did I—?

NORA

You had your own child, but you left her
to raise another mother's child.
You chose to love someone's child who wasn't your own.
And that's okay.
But don't tell me we're different.
We're the same.

ANNE MARIE

No. We're not.
I didn't have a father with money like you had a father with money,
I didn't have the same options you had.
Do you think I wanted to leave my home and become a nanny?
My options were—what—working in a factory and wearing my
body down to the point of uselessness at an early age,
or I could go out and be a prostitute

NORA

Yes. No, I— You're right.

ANNE MARIE

I would have never, ever left my child if I didn't absolutely have
to.

NORA

But I did.

And you may not believe me but
I *had* to leave . . .

. . . and leaving my children was the hardest part—
it's the part of what I did that I hate the most,
that hurts, that still hurts—
don't you think there wasn't a moment that I

didn't think of sending them a little letter,
a little note saying "hello, mommy is thinking of you,
mommy loves you, mommy misses you very very much,"

or on a birthday or Christmas sending a gift—
I did—I bought them gifts, Anne Marie,
for the first couple of years—
I had a little pile of gifts for them sitting in the corner of my room,
I'd buy these gifts and I'd be just about to send them—
and then I wouldn't because I knew
that sending them would make *me* feel very good,
but for them it could be—
because I thought about them thinking about me,
thinking that they must wonder about me,
and thinking that I wanted to answer all of their questions—

Better for there to be nothing,
for there to be silence,
than this thing that's somewhere halfway in between because

that—*that* Anne Marie—would be cruel.

A wound has to be allowed to heal,
no matter how much you have the desire,
the urge to touch it, to—

It's not good for the . . . the healing.
Do you understand?

Do you.

ANNE MARIE

. . .

NORA

What I did wasn't easy.
It was hard.
It took discipline.
And I had to think past the feelings
and about what's best for everyone involved.

And yes, yes!—because of what you did,
because of what you gave up,
my children felt loved.

And I am grateful.
You say I'm not, but I am.
And I'm so sorry if
I did not make you feel that.

(A moment of silence.)

Anne Marie, I have money,
and I can give you a kind of freedom.
I can buy you your own house.
I can give you a lump sum of money so that—provided you invest
it wisely—you'll never need to work again. You're on some kind
of—I'm sure—tiny allowance, trickling out just enough money
to get you to the end of the month.

Isn't that true.

And I look at you, and you look so tired and worn,
and when you walk, you limp.
And you say you have problems with your stomach?
And in exchange Torvald gives you a little room in the back?

I can give you a better life,
and I promise you, it's not conditional.
You help me or not,
that's up to you.

ANNE MARIE

. . .

NORA

Can I do that for you?
Will you let me do that?

ANNE MARIE

. . .

NORA

. . .

ANNE MARIE

. . . No. I don't want your money.
It's too late in life to up and . . .

NORA

. . .

ANNE MARIE

Option three.

NORA

What?

ANNE MARIE

Option three. You said you were looking for a third option for
handling the problem with Torvald?

I know a third option.
Would you like to know what it is.

NORA

Uh, yes.

ANNE MARIE

It means you have to do the thing I think you're most scared to
do, but if you want what you want—

NORA

what is it.

ANNE MARIE

Meet your daughter.

NORA

. . . no

ANNE MARIE

wait—

NORA

it's not a good idea—

ANNE MARIE

hear me out.

NORA

I'm like a stranger to her—

ANNE MARIE

Listen: you were not able to convince Torvald
to agree to the divorce.
And I would never be able to convince him either.
Our words mean nothing to him—

But Emmy—she can be very persuasive,
—I think you'll be impressed—
you know I raised her to be very resourceful,
just like I raised you, and I think maybe—
maybe she would have a good idea for what could be done.

NORA

I think that could be very confusing, the way things are—
there's a balance that we have that I wouldn't want to upset

ANNE MARIE

but she's an adult,
there's no damage you can do,
not now. She has a life—
a life outside of you,
and she's happy with that life,
I think you aggrandize yourself.

NORA

. . .

ANNE MARIE

Hey. I have nothing to gain from you meeting with her or not.
You ask me what will get you what you're looking for.
This is what will do it.

It's the only option.

Emmy

Emmy enters.

EMMY

Hello.

I'm Emmy.

I'm your daughter.

NORA

Yes, I know.

EMMY

It's very nice to meet you.

NORA

You too.

EMMY

. . .

NORA

I hope you're all right with this

EMMY

with this?

NORA

Meeting me, I hope it isn't strange
or upsetting—

EMMY

no, not at all

NORA

good.

I was worried it would be.

EMMY

Why?

NORA

Well I've never been part of your life.

EMMY

This counts as being part of my life—?

NORA

no but a little step towards—seems potentially,
I don't know, harmful,
I don't want to do any harm.

(Emmy thinks about this for a moment, like she's adding something up in her mind, and then . . .)

EMMY

No I don't think us doing this—meeting—I don't think it does any harm

NORA

okay, well—good—I hope—

EMMY

and just so you know, I feel no animosity towards you.

NORA

Oh that's—that's nice to hear

EMMY

this is exciting!—meeting you is

NORA

yes

EMMY

I don't remember you at all

NORA

I didn't think that you would.
You were very little, very—

EMMY

for the longest time I thought you were dead

NORA

well you're not the first person to tell me that

> EMMY

everyone thought you died,
everyone in town, everyone who—

> NORA

I didn't

> EMMY

except obviously
Torvald, Anne Marie,
my brothers—but I did for a long time—

> NORA

so when did you—?

> EMMY

when I was seven or eight—

> NORA

I see

> EMMY

my brothers told me.
They remembered things that I didn't or couldn't,
and they told me about how you left.
I didn't believe them at first—sounded
like the kind of thing you say to
avoid telling a kid the harder truth,
but Ivar said that if I didn't believe them,
that I could go down to the clerk's office
where they keep all the records—birth records, death
records—
and he said that if I looked for your death certificate
there wouldn't be one

—and I went to school with a boy whose
father worked in the clerk's office,
and this boy liked me, so I acted like I liked him back,
and got him to let me into the office one night.
And I looked through the records,
and there was no death certificate,
and then I knew, that
you weren't dead,
you just left.

Bob and Ivar told me that some day maybe you'd come back
and that I should be ready for it, that you would come
and that you would take us with you,
and that you would be a lot more fun to live with than Torvald
who—he's not bad—but fun isn't the word I'd use to describe—

NORA

yes—

EMMY

I mean I think it's kind of adorable—his sort of—I don't know
what to call it

NORA

gloom?—

EMMY

no—that's not quite . . .

Bob remembered you best

NORA

oh Bob.

EMMY

Bob missed you the most.

Bob could draw.

I asked Bob if he would draw a picture of you—he wouldn't.

Ivar said that it was probably because if he did,

Bob would start crying

and Bob never liked to be seen crying

because he thought crying made his face look fat.

NORA

Yes,

I do remember that about Bob

about him—not the fat face thing—but the crying—he doesn't

still do that—?

EMMY

he does

NORA

poor Bob

EMMY

Ivar on the other hand—

NORA

the opposite of Bob

EMMY

in every way

NORA

yes.

EMMY

Now tell me something you remember about me.

NORA

You

EMMY

yes!

NORA

. . . uhhhhh, what should I—well here's something:
When you were born

EMMY

yes—?

NORA

I had you very fast.
You came right out of me—like you were racing to get out
into the world—like you couldn't wait— The boys—they were
very slow. I was in labor for—oh god, it was terrible—
but you were very easy.

So. You can put that into your
book of memories.

EMMY

. . . And tell me something about you.

NORA

Uh like what?

EMMY

Oh I don't know—

Are you happy?

NORA

Yes.

Very.

EMMY

What makes you happy?

NORA

My work makes me happy.
I like my house, I have a nice little house,
it's by a lake,
it's quiet.

EMMY

That sounds nice . . .

NORA

And are you happy, Emmy?

EMMY

I am.

NORA

What makes you happy.

EMMY

All sorts of things:
I have enough money.
I have enough food.
Physically I'm
fine—there aren't problems
with my health.

NORA

That's good.

EMMY

I actually think in a lot of ways
things turned out better because you weren't around.

NORA

. . .

EMMY

I think I'm better at life because of it.
I had a lot more responsibility,
I had to deal with some difficult truths about life
at an earlier age than you usually have to
deal with those types of things.

I feel bad for the kids who growing up had the usual life.
I feel special.

NORA

. . . that's good to hear, it's—I'm happy that—

EMMY

people say I'm an old soul.

NORA

yes, yes!—you seem very
grown up. Very adult. Very
impressive.

EMMY

(*Smiling to herself*) Thank you.

And you, you've done well because of it too, haven't you

NORA

what do you mean—?

                    EMMY

Anne Marie told me that you have your own money,
and that you write books.

                    NORA

I do.

                    EMMY

I find that very interesting.

                    NORA

I'll send you one.

                    EMMY

I don't really read books.

                    NORA

No?

                    EMMY

Never could get interested in—I get bored easily—it's . . .

                    NORA

. . . And so, Emmy—

                    EMMY

yes—?

                    NORA

did Anne Marie also tell you *why* I'm here?

                    EMMY

All I know is—

that you and Torvald were supposed to be divorced
but you found out you're not,

and you're trying to get Torvald to file the divorce
but he won't do it

NORA

that's pretty much it.

EMMY

I'm guessing what you want from me is for me to go to him
and convince him to do the thing that he's refusing to do

NORA

yes, yes, that's—I was just thinking that
if you were to go to him,
tell him that this is what's right for him—

EMMY

uh-huh

NORA

for everyone,
tell him it will be all right,
that there's no point in wrecking everything he's built,
tell him to do it for you

EMMY

but it's not for me

NORA

of course it's for you—
the whole family
and you and Bob and Ivar and—
the kind of—I don't know—disgrace
that could come as a result of—
—it would make the family look very bad—and

I don't know if Anne Marie told you, but there's this judge
who's threatening to—

EMMY

yes, I know

NORA

right. so.

EMMY

. . .

NORA

I understand if maybe you have concerns.

Let me try to address some of—maybe you're not sure
how to approach this matter with Torvald,
I understand that, yes, that could be awkward: what do you say?
You go to him out of the blue:
I think you should give Nora the divorce she's asking for—
he'll think you talked with me and that I put you up to it

EMMY

but aren't you—?

NORA

what—

EMMY

putting me up to it.

NORA

So say instead—you don't tell him we met,
and say instead that you heard from
Anne Marie about my problem—well, you did—
that's true—Anne Marie told you what she told you,

and say you got to thinking about the situation
and my dilemma and what this could mean to Torvald,
and how it could look really bad,
get him in a bad spot with his reputation—
and explain to him how you think it's best
to just let me go
and let it all go
and file the divorce.

If you can show him how he's making this worse for himself,
if you leave me out of it,
because I don't think Torvald will do what Torvald does
for my sake, that his interests are—

EMMY

are what? What do you think his interests—?

NORA

Honestly?

Isn't it apparent?

I think he doesn't want to let me go,
that there's some part of him that is hoping
that maybe I'd come back to him, that there
would be uh reconciliation.

EMMY

Did he propose a reconciliation?

NORA

. . .

EMMY

. . .

NORA

. . . um—

EMMY

No, see, I think you're very wrong,
and that you've made a lot of assumptions
and that you don't know what you're doing,
you think you do, but you—and it's not your fault,
but I need to correct you—

NORA

correct me—?

EMMY

Torvald did something really stupid.

I know that he's still, technically speaking, married to you.
And I'm not saying that none of this is his fault.
There's fault on his part, for sure.
But basically, what happened,
when you left, people noticed,
and of course they noticed,
and people would ask, "Where's Nora?"
And Torvald, I'm sure you could guess,
he was pretty upset about it, felt pretty private about it,
didn't want to talk about it—it was embarrassing—people ask
him where you are and he'd have to say you left him—it would
be awkward, both for him and for the person asking,
so at first when people asked, he'd say that you had gone away,
left town, visiting family,
something like that.

He really didn't say much about it, he didn't want to lie,
but then when about two or so months had gone by,

and you were still gone—I mean I don't know
exactly how it happened,
obviously I was so little, I
wasn't aware of what was happening—but
someone made the assumption that you weren't well,
that you had gotten sick,
and Torvald didn't say no,
so that's the story that went around—
that you were gone and you were sick
and recovering at a sanitarium.
And then another month or two passes,
and someone somewhere says something or makes the assumption
that it's worse than that,
and that you hadn't recovered
and you were
no longer alive.

And that's what people assumed,
and Torvald—now he's so far in
and to explain the truth—I know it's a weak thing he did
but he had his job at the bank and was
a very respected member of the community,
very well-liked, trusted,
to have to explain such an embarrassing set of
truths and misunderstandings and so on—
so he said nothing.
And by saying nothing
he was sort of saying something
which is that you
had died.

And once people came to think that,
that's when—well you know what happens when that happens—
there's an outpouring of affection and support,

people visited,
they brought food,
they really rallied around him
and us—the whole family.

And there's also some government support for the families,
there's that—some money you get—of course there
was no death certificate ever filed,
but these things happen, mistakes, oversights—
just because of the way people found out,
this gradual sort of realization that that's what was—and because
Torvald is well-respected, well-liked, and because he runs the
bank—

You see?

It's a problem. You being here, doing what you're doing.

Do you—?

                    NORA
No, I don't—

                    EMMY
It's fraud, technically, it is—it's fraud, and Torvald could be tried—
he could lose everything—just like you, and that's why
he can't give you your divorce.

                    NORA
. . .

                    EMMY
But . . .

there is another option:

NORA

. . .

EMMY

You die.

NORA

What?

EMMY

Let me ask you:
who have you seen while you've been in town?
me, Anne Marie, Torvald . . .

anyone else?

NORA

. . . no.

EMMY

Good.

Remember how I said there's no death certificate?
What if there was one. What if—using what connections I have—
that piece of paper were to just show up in the files of the local
clerk's office?

You see?

If you're dead, there is no marriage.

NORA

Does Torvald know about this idea?

                              EMMY

No.

This is my idea.

I came up with it myself.

                              NORA

. . .

                              EMMY

It's clever, isn't it.

                              NORA

It is.

                              EMMY

Thank you.

So will you do it then?

                              NORA

. . .

                              EMMY

Will you—what reason would you have for not doing it.

I can't think of one, can you?

                              NORA

You'd be committing forgery

                              EMMY

yes

                              NORA

of public records

EMMY

sure, but—

NORA

the kind of trouble, you'd—

EMMY

no one will find out

NORA

I do have some experience with this kind of thing, and you'd be
surprised by how these kinds of things can just sorta come to
light, at the worst possible—

EMMY

but if Torvald's lie is exposed—

NORA

How is this right!

How is it right that Torvald lies
and I'm the one paying for it—
that you're paying for it—
that—and I'm expected to be the one to lose everything because—

EMMY

It's just that I'm engaged.

NORA

. . . ah.

EMMY

To a man.

NORA

I see.

EMMY

Named Jorgen.

NORA

. . . Jorgen.

EMMY

He's a banker

NORA

of course he is

EMMY

he works with Torvald.

NORA

. . .

EMMY

And if you cause a scandal he won't be able to marry me.

And there goes my future.

Gone.

NORA

. . .

EMMY

You don't like that, do you

NORA

what

EMMY

that I'm getting married.

You think no one should get married

NORA

no, I—

EMMY

Anne Marie told me.
She told me, "Don't bring up Jorgen."
But it seemed weird not to tell you,
because we're in love.
I know you probably don't believe in "being in love."

NORA

But I do. I do believe in—
I have nothing against love, Emmy, but
love
love is different from marriage.
Marriage is this binding contract,
and love is—love has to be the opposite of a contract—
love needs to be free,
and it is free
until the moment you marry,
and then something changes
and you're no longer as free as you once were—
because you go from being two separate people
to something more like one person,
and you get swallowed up—and because of the way the world is—
it's *you* that's going to get swallowed up into him.
And anything you want
for yourself will have to be part of what he wants,
and he's going to expect this from you

EMMY

Jorgen is very kind, very—

NORA

so was Torvald—has nothing to do with
kindness—it has to do with . . .
what people do and have always done and
don't even bother to question—
How much do you even know about marriage?

EMMY

Nothing

NORA

exactly

EMMY

because you left, I know nothing about
what a marriage is and what it looks like.

But I do know what the absence of it looks like,
and what I want is the opposite of that.

I want to be held.
I want to be possessed.
I want to be somebody's something—
I can see you cringe when I say what I'm saying.
But that's about you, and it's not about me,
and I'm telling you what I want,
and you may want something different for yourself,
but don't make my wants about your wants

NORA

but—

EMMY

you're telling me I don't want what I want?

NORA

Emmy, I'm telling you that I once wanted what you wanted
only to find out that when I got what I wanted
that it was definitely not what I wanted.

EMMY

But you don't know that it will be the same with me.
I'm not you.

NORA

I have a feeling you're a lot like me

EMMY

no

NORA

the kinds of things you're saying
are the kinds of things I said

EMMY

You don't even know me.
You came back here for the first time in fifteen years
and you didn't want to see me—the only reason you're even
talking to me is because you want something from me

NORA

no, no

EMMY

that's not why you wanted to see me?

NORA

. . .

EMMY

. . .

NORA

Yes, yes I did come here to ask you for some help

EMMY

see—

NORA

but you think I didn't *want* to see you—?

EMMY

you don't ask me any questions

NORA

because I don't know where to begin!

EMMY

How do you think it makes me feel
to know that the only reason my mother
wants to see me is to get me to fix a problem for her.

NORA

. . .

EMMY

. . .

NORA

. . .

EMMY

You've never given me anything.
This is the only thing I'm asking for

NORA

you'd be putting yourself at terrible risk

EMMY

and what about you—?
you talk to me about the trouble I could get into by forging a
death certificate—I'd imagine the trouble you're facing is worse.
Aren't you scared?

NORA

What scares me more is the thought of you doing everything
that I did
that I wish I didn't do—

That's worse because it means that everything I've done since
walking out that door
means nothing

EMMY

everything you've done, which is—what?

NORA

The books, the books I've written—everything that I—

EMMY

these books that tell women to leave their marriages

NORA

if they're feeling stuck and—

EMMY

and they do—?

NORA

some are moved to—

EMMY

and how is that good?

How many women have left their husbands because of you?
How many women have left their children?
How many women have left their husbands and children, and
gotten themselves into the same kind of trouble you're in right
now?— It's—it's like you've saved everyone from a drowning
boat, but you've left them with no way to get back to shore.

NORA

. . .

EMMY

I actually think it's good to be stuck in a marriage.
It's the fact that we're bound together, that it's difficult to leave,
that actually makes people stick around and try—
I think—because if things keep on going
the way you say they should,
then—what will that look like?—
a future where everyone is leaving each other—
that in a lifetime one person will have tried to be with—what,
four, five, six people—but always just skating through their
lives, never able to settle or slow or experience
anything that takes any real difficult time—

never finding a home,
never finding a place to rest,
a person to rest with,
never finding a person who knows you
and that sounds—and what do I know,
but that sounds so sad
and so lonely
and so

so deeply unsatisfying
this future
where we're all just nomads . . .

Is that really what you want?

NORA

. . .

EMMY

You let me do this for you—Nora Helmer will officially be dead.
You leave here,
you move somewhere quiet—you stay quiet for a couple of years,
this trouble with the judge, it will eventually pass,
and then you'll be free—
free of Nora Helmer. That's what you always wanted
from the very beginning, isn't it?
When you walked out that door,
you wanted to find out who you really were.
You've found that person.
You don't need Nora Helmer anymore.
She's dead.
And now you really get to be reborn as
this new person you've created.
And me and Torvald and my brothers can go on
living lives without you.

(*An unusually long period of silence.*)

NORA

. . .

EMMY

. . .

NORA

. . .

EMMY

. . .

NORA

. . .

EMMY

Nora . . . ?

NORA

This isn't right—
this scheming,
this lying—this is what I left behind—

EMMY

. . .

NORA

. . .

(Nora begins to leave.)

EMMY

where are you going?

NORA

You think I've never given you anything, but
you don't know what I've given you—
because what I'm trying to do for you—
the kind of world I'm trying make for you—
it hasn't happened yet.

But it won't happen this way—not if I let you or Torvald
fix this problem for me

EMMY

. . .

NORA

no, I have to do this myself—
If that judge wants me to publish a letter,
then I'll do it and I'll tell everyone
"yes, yes, I'm a criminal,
and I am not sorry,"
I'll go and face the people who are telling me what I can and
can't do and show them that there's nothing they can do—

EMMY

they can put you in prison—

NORA

it doesn't matter—because I'm already
in a prison if I'm having to rely on Torvald to give me a divorce,
if I'm having to hide behind some pseudonym
if I'm—if we're beholden to all of these

bad rules is what they are—

there are so many bad rules in this world, Emmy,
I'm not going to follow these bad rules,
this is my chance to change the rules

because twenty, thirty years from now
the world isn't going to be the kind of place I say it's going to be
unless I'm the one to make it that way—

(Anne Marie enters with Torvald.
Torvald is bleeding from the head.)

ANNE MARIE

Torvald's been attacked!—

EMMY

What—?

ANNE MARIE

just found him like this walking through the streets like this, like
a crazy person—

EMMY

I'll go get some bandages

(Emmy exits.)

ANNE MARIE

blood coming out of his head, people on the street staring at
him—
(To Torvald) everyone's going to think you've gone out of your
mind—
(To Nora) this is all your fault—none of this would have happened if you didn't come here—I should have never answered
your letter, I should have never said it was all right for you to
come here—

(Emmy reenters with supplies.)

TORVALD

Anne Marie

why don't you—I don't know—take a walk.

ANNE MARIE

. . .

(Anne Marie exits.
For a moment, Emmy dresses Torvald's wounds.
Then . . .)

TORVALD

Emmy, you too.

(Emmy exits.)

(To Nora) We should talk—

Nora
& Torvald

Torvald produces a book.

NORA

. . .

TORVALD

. . .

NORA

I see.

TORVALD

Anne Marie told me that you—you write these little books—

NORA

little—

TORVALD

I didn't mean that in a—I meant—just she told me that that's
what you do now,

so I was curious,

and I walked into a bookstore.
I asked the man in the bookstore
what's the book that the women are reading,
I'd like to read that book,
and he said, well you must be thinking of this book,
and he handed me a book,
and it didn't have your name on it,
but I figured it was a uh—

NORA

pseudonym

TORVALD

Right. Yes.
And so I bought the book,
and I took it with me to the fjord,

and I sat on the rock,
and I read the book,
the whole thing,
from beginning to end.

And the book was about you,
and the book was about me,
and it was about all the things that happened between us.

It was hard for me to read it

NORA

it was hard for me to live it.

TORVALD

. . . I'm sitting there reading
and thinking every so often,
oh I remember that or I forgot that or—

And some things made me really mad and—

NORA

like what?

TORVALD

I come off pretty badly in the book. I come off as a real—

I'm going to read some parts out loud

NORA

just say what you—

TORVALD

"He looked at me with a look of condescension"

(Turns a page.)

—you say things like that often—"He sneered,"
"He pontificated" . . .

but this is the one.
This one is the one that really—

(Turns to a page.)

"I lived in terror of my husband.
He didn't so much look *at* me, as much as he looked *through* me.
I didn't exist.
Yes, he doted on me,
but he only doted because the act of doting made him feel good.
But you could have substituted in for me
any woman. It didn't matter.

Once I asked him what he liked about me.
He told me he liked everything.
I pressed for more.
He said I was pretty.
He said I was his.
He said I was perfect.

This is why I lived in terror.
Not because he was violent—he wasn't—
not because he ever threatened my life—he never did—
unless you count living with someone who can't see you
as life-threatening—which in a way it is."

NORA

. . .

TORVALD

That hurts.

NORA

Because . . . ?

TORVALD

I'm not like that—not *now*

NORA

it's not about how you are now. It's about how—

TORVALD

I think about dying.

I uh think about how when I die—
which will be some day sooner than later—
and I think what it is I'm leaving behind—what mark I've made—
and I think about how this is it.

(To the book) This is the story that's told about me and that's it,
and I don't want that to be it,
and so—

NORA

. . .

TORVALD

I went to the clerk's office this morning

NORA

you did

TORVALD

told the clerk,
"I'm here to file a divorce—"

NORA

oh Torvald—

TORVALD

let me finish—he didn't understand because—

NORA

he thought I was dead.

TORVALD

Oh, you know about the—

NORA

yes—

TORVALD

he thought I was crazy,
he said, "Torvald, you think you've seen a ghost."
I said no, I said, "I've been lying,
there's a pile of lies, I've been lying,
and that's done, I won't lie,
I'll face the consequences."

I even said, "If you don't believe me, find the death certificate,"
and he said if there's no death certificate then
he should go ahead and make one.

And here he is taking out the papers to
write up a death certificate,
and it was as if he was about to end your life in front my eyes—

NORA

and did he?

TORVALD

No, I grabbed the pen from his hand,
and in grabbing the pen, I knocked him to the ground,

and this clerk, he's not a small man—
he's younger than me, stronger than me—

and he grabs me, he holds me down,
and I—I'm just fighting back,
trying to break free of him.

And this fight—it's now—it's bigger than itself,
and I'm fighting for my life—
and he pushes me, and I fall . . .

my head hits the ground, where there's a bit of stone.
It cut into my head, I could hear the skull crack—

and he's now horrified, he backs away, I think he's even crying,
he says, "Torvald Helmer, what have you turned into,
what are you?"

And I said to him, said to the clerk,
"You will give me my divorce,"
and he nodded his head,
because he understood,
that this was about more than it was about.

He could have had me locked up,
but he understood, and—

(Torvald takes out a paper.)

This is it.

I did this for you.
I made everything right
by ruining myself,
by exposing a pile of lies that I've been hiding for fifteen years,
and I'll probably lose my job
and lose my friends
and lose my savings,
but I did it
so hopefully I won't be remembered
the way you remember me
when I'm gone.

You can even go
and write a new book
where I'm a better man.

(Nora looks at the paper.)

Here. Take it.

(Nora does not take it.)

You won't take it.

NORA

Thank you.

Thank you, Torvald.

I appreciate that you did this . . .

but . . .

I don't need this anymore

TORVALD

what

NORA

the divorce, I don't need it.

But I really do appreciate that you—

TORVALD

I CAN'T WIN WITH YOU!

NORA

. . .

TORVALD

. . .

NORA

. . .

TORVALD

I CAN'T WIN WITH YOU!

I CAN'T FUCKING WIN WITH YOU

NORA

THERE'S NOTHING TO WIN!
STOP TRYING TO "WIN"!

TORVALD

I'M JUST TRYING TO BE A GOOD GUY HERE

NORA

YOU GO AND YOU MAKE EVERYTHING ABOUT YOU—

YOU EVEN MADE MY BOOK ABOUT YOU

TORVALD

I'M IN THERE AREN'T I?

NORA

IT'S *MY* BOOK, *MY* FEELINGS, *MY* THOUGHTS,
MY EXPERIENCE, *MY* LIFE—

TORVALD

I GAVE YOU WHAT YOU WANTED!

NORA

ONLY BECAUSE YOU WANTED TO LOOK GOOD—

TORVALD

YOU WERE IN TROUBLE!

NORA

BECAUSE OF YOU—BECAUSE OF YOUR LIES, / YOUR COWARDLY—

TORVALD

YOU WERE IN TROUBLE AND I SAVED / YOU AND—

NORA

I DON'T NEED A FUCKING SAVIOR—

TORVALD

YOU HAVE NO IDEA WHAT THIS COST ME—

NORA

YOU HAVE NO IDEA WHAT THIS COST ME!

TORVALD

NOW I'M RUINED BECAUSE I TRIED TO DO THE RIGHT / THING—

NORA

I BET YOU *WANTED* TO BE RUINED

TORVALD

THAT'S INSANE!

NORA

YOU LOVE IT WHEN PEOPLE FEEL BAD FOR YOU—

TORVALD

/ AW FUCK YOU—

NORA

HAVE TO TAKE CARE OF YOU, NURSE YOU BACK TO HEALTH—THAT'S YOUR WHOLE LIFE—EVERYONE

GIVING UP EVERYTHING FOR TORVALD—SAME THING AS ALWAYS—YOU HAVEN'T CHANGED A BIT.

(A long silence.)

TORVALD

. . .

NORA

. . .

TORVALD

. . .

NORA

. . .

TORVALD

. . .

NORA

. . .

TORVALD

. . .

NORA

. . .

TORVALD

. . .

NORA

. . .

(And then . . .)

TORVALD

. . . I don't know what to do around you,
I don't know how to behave . . .

NORA

. . .

TORVALD

. . .

NORA

. . .

(And then . . .)

TORVALD

What happened—you used to be so—you were a different person and I find it incredibly disturbing that when I look at you
I can't even see inside there to see
the person that I used to know.

(Silence, and then . . .)

I think I miss you, Nora.

NORA

. . .

TORVALD

You think I don't see you,
that I don't know who you are,
but I don't know—I think maybe the same way

I made assumptions about you,
you made assumptions about me.
And maybe I would like what you really are,
and maybe I didn't like the things you thought I liked,
and kind of found some of them pretty annoying.

I don't know.

It's just so hard

NORA

what's so—?

TORVALD

all of this.
Being with people.

NORA

Yes.

TORVALD

Does it have to be so hard, really?

. . .

NORA

. . .

TORVALD

. . .

NORA

. . .

TORVALD

. . .

NORA

. . .

TORVALD

. . . you said there have been others since me.

NORA

There were.

TORVALD

Who were they?

NORA

All sorts of people.
Some were important,
some weren't.
Some stand out in my mind,
and some sort of just fade.

TORVALD

. . .

NORA

There was a painter,

and there was another banker,

there was an architect.

And there was also the man who built the houses the architect
designed.

There was . . . there was a man, a very young man.
I thought it would be interesting,
to have a relationship with a very young man

TORVALD

was it—?

NORA

no.

TORVALD

. . .

NORA

. . .

TORVALD

There was a woman—

NORA

there was?

TORVALD

Don't be so surprised.

NORA

. . .

TORVALD

She was a widow—used to live three houses down.
After her husband died,
she'd come over for dinner and we'd play cards.

NORA

Who was it—? Sofia?

                    TORVALD

Yes—

                    NORA

her?

                    TORVALD

What.

(Nora laughs.)

What.

                    NORA

I just can't picture it.
I'm *trying*.
I just—can't picture it.

                    TORVALD

Kids liked her,
she liked the kids,
but I just couldn't because—
because I was afraid.

                    NORA

. . .

                    TORVALD

. . .

                    NORA

. . .

                    TORVALD

You say you've become so honest.
So be honest with me:

I'm talking about two people,
spending time together,
figuring out
how to be around each other.

Is that a true marriage?
Before you walked out that door, I remember, that's
what you said you wanted.

So? Have you ever experienced that with anyone?

Be honest with me.

NORA

. . .

TORVALD

. . .

NORA

No.

TORVALD

I haven't either,
and I don't want to die
having never had that experience.

NORA

Then go have it.
I want you to have that.

TORVALD

But what about you?

NORA

. . . when I left here, Torvald
fifteen years ago,
the first thing I did
—because I had nothing: no home, no family, no money—
was I went and lived in a boarding house.
And because I had no real skills other than I could sew things—
I did that—and made money sewing
and bit by bit saved up what I could—

Because what I really wanted to do was,
for the first time in my life,
be by myself.

So when I saved enough money,
I left the boarding house,
and went and lived up north.
I found what was basically an abandoned shack.

And even though I was living by myself—
for everything I did—
every decision I made,
from what I ate to when I went to bed—
I could hear a voice in the back of my head
that either sounded like you or my father or the pastor or
any number of other people I knew—
I'd always in my head somehow manage to
check with that person
to see what he thought,
even though that person wasn't a person
but my thinking of that person.

And so, as long as that continued,
I'd decided that I'd live in silence,

not speaking and
avoiding the speaking of others—

and I'd live like this until
I couldn't remember what other people sounded like—
until I no longer heard a voice in my head
other than my voice
or what I was certain had to be my voice.

That was almost two years,

two years of silence.

And once I could hear my voice,
I could think of things that I wanted
that had nothing to do with what anyone else wanted.

It's really hard to hear your own voice,
and every lie you tell
makes your voice harder to hear,
and a lot of what we do is lying.
Especially when what we want so badly
from other people
is for them to love us.

So I find that I'm best—that I'm my best self if I'm by myself.

TORVALD

. . .

NORA

. . . but it's nice to sit with you.

TORVALD

Yes.
It is.

(Torvald gently squeezes Nora's hand.
And holds it there for a bit.
And then . . .)

NORA

Alright.

I'm ready.

TORVALD

For what.

NORA

I'm ready to go.
I'm ready to do this again—walk out that door
and away from this house,
off into the—
and I know that I'm going to have to fight a lot of people
all over again
and harder than I did before,

and I might lose everything I have,
but I've done that before
and I can do it again—

(A beat.
And then Nora gets up.
Nora and Torvald walk to the door together.
Nora begins to exit then turns around in the doorway.)

The world didn't change as much as I thought it would,

but I know that some day everything will be different,
and everyone will be free—freer than they are now.

TORVALD

I can't imagine that.

NORA

Yeah . . . well

I just hope I live to see it.

(Nora walks out the door.
Torvald watches.
Door shuts, lights out.)

END OF PLAY

REBECCA MARTINEZ

LUCAS HNATH's plays include *A Doll's House, Part 2* (eight Tony Award nominations, including Best Play); *Hillary and Clinton*; *Red Speedo*; *The Christians*; *A Public Reading of an Unproduced Screenplay about the Death of Walt Disney*; *Isaac's Eye*; and *Death Tax*. He has been produced on Broadway at the John Golden Theatre, Off-Broadway at New York Theatre Workshop, Playwrights Horizons, Soho Rep, and Ensemble Studio Theatre. His plays have been produced nationally and internationally with premieres at the Humana Festival of New Plays, Victory Gardens, and South Coast Rep. He has been a resident playwright at New Dramatists since 2011. His awards include the Kesselring Prize, a Guggenheim Fellowship, the Whiting Award, two Steinberg/ATCA New Play Award Citations, the Steinberg Playwright Award, an Edgerton Foundation New Play Award, the Outer Critics Circle Award for Best New Play, an Obie, and the Windham-Campbell Prize.